Tray-Sean Ben Salmi aka T7

It Starts with You!

–

Anything Is Possible!

Tray-Sean Ben Salmi aka T7

TEDx Speaker

Tray-Sean Ben Salmi aka T7

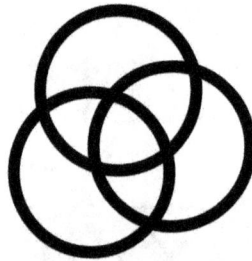

Influencer
PUBLISHING

Changing the world one mind at a time

Published By
Influencer Publishing™

ISBN: **978-1-913310-60-8**

DEDICATION

This book is dedicated to individuals who desire to achieve and take their lives to the next level. There is a saying that it all starts with one single step, but in my view that is a flawed premise because without direction you will never achieve what you set out to. So, I like to say that success begins with a single step in the right direction. Learn to live life with purpose, have big dreams and smaller objectives along the way and most of all understand that you are not a product of your circumstances - you are a product of the decisions that you choose to make on a daily basis.

It all starts with you! Come join me along this journey as we cover some motivational words that can help you to make your dreams a reality. I need you to understand that some desired outcomes may be easier than others. If you want to live tomorrow like most people don't, then you will have to be willing to do the things that most people won't and with that said let's begin.

It Starts with You! – Anything Is Possible!

ACKNOWLEDGMENTS

Just before I start, I would like to take a moment to acknowledge my amazing family, friends and those who have supported me along the way.

My mum (Sabrina Ben Salmi), my stepfather (Mohamed Ben Salmi), my nana (Mary Paul), my elder sister (Lashai Ben Salmi), my sister (Yasmine), my brother (Paolo), my youngest brother (Amire Ben Salmi), my Abuelo (Alan Shelton), my Abuela (Justine Shelton), Ras Al, Lesley Warren, Ben Green, Dani Barahona, Pastor Mo, Steve & Marjorie Foundation and Rev Trevor Adams to name a few.

It Starts with You! – Anything Is Possible!

CONTENTS

It Starts with You! – Anything Is Possible!

INTRODUCTION

Hi there, my name is Tray-Sean Ben Salmi aka T7. I wrote this book to motivate you to keep pushing, to keep persevering and to keep striving to reach your goals when you feel like quitting. Stop comparing yourself to others, your only competition is with the person who you were yesterday. Push yourself to become at least 1% better each and every day and eventually you'll be sure to get there. Remember that failure isn't fatal, the same way that success isn't eternal so keep grinding.

I hope you enjoy this book!!

It Starts with You! – Anything Is Possible!

MOTIVATIONAL
WORDS

"TEAMWORK MAKES THE DREAMWORK."

"TEAMWORK MAKES THE DREAMWORK."

One thing that often has more of an effect than we realise. is when it comes to achieving your goal. Is who you surround yourself with, be it friends, family etc because they influence your mindset, habits, behaviour, drive and perspective among many other things. So, become more aware and conscious of the people you allow in your circle as if you were to take a look at your circle right now and not get inspired or feel motivated in some way then you have a cage not a circle. Now that's not to say that you are better than them or vice versa it's simply to say that you do not match, think of it like a puzzle and they aren't the right puzzle piece.

"WORKING HARD WILL ONLY HELP IF YOU ARE GOING IN THE RIGHT DIRECTION SO WORK SMART CONSISTENTLY."

"WORKING HARD WILL ONLY HELP IF YOU ARE GOING IN THE RIGHT DIRECTION SO WORK SMART CONSISTENTLY."

Success always leaves clues… No matter what you aim to achieve, someone else has already attained it. People tend to overcomplicate things which often leads to them giving up just before the glory. Instead of rushing into things without a plan, without taking a breath, learn to take a step back to analyse the situation at hand and think of the easiest way to achieve your goal. Start by getting clear on your goal then work back slowly and develop a list of objectives you want to accomplish in between to make that big dream achievable.

"IF YOU SIT IN A CHAIR LONG ENOUGH, YOU'LL FORGET WHAT IT FEELS LIKE TO STAND..."

It Starts with You! – Anything Is Possible!

"IF YOU SIT IN A CHAIR LONG ENOUGH YOU'LL FORGET WHAT IT FEELS LIKE TO STAND..."

What do I mean by this?

Think of the chair as your comfort zone and if you stay there for long enough, if you stay in that seat for long enough you will become oblivious to the power that you harness, to achieve your desired outcomes and to think outside the box.

At the end of the day when it comes to certain things in life it's about thinking about the impact. Take small consistent steps, and more importantly

It Starts with You! – Anything Is Possible!

so start today. For instance, when it comes to investing this very effect which we call compound interest can work both with you or against so it's up to you to decide. Either way remember that you're creating your future whether it's one you desire or not depends entirely on what decisions you are making.

So, choose wisely!

"WHATEVER YOU'RE NOT CHANGING YOU ARE CHOOSING."

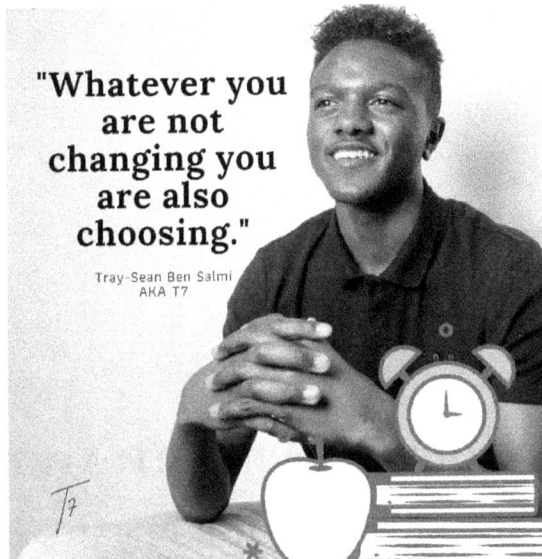

"Whatever you are not changing you are also choosing."

Tray-Sean Ben Salmi
AKA T7

Sometimes the smallest things can change our lives in the blink of an eye, but what matters is what you take from that experience and simply learning to accept it for what it is.

You see sometimes, we actually make things seem a lot more complex than they actually are. You may even be unconsciously stopping yourself from growing... from achieving... from success.

Learn to trust the process and you'll get there in the end.

"YOUR CURRENT SITUATION IS NOT YOUR FINAL DESTINATION."

"YOUR CURRENT SITUATION IS NOT YOUR FINAL DESTINATION."

You can't become who you want to be because you are too attached to who you have been.

The secret to change is to focus all of your energy on building the new, not fighting to stay with the old.

In life we often get caught up in our past problems and we often lose our vision and at times we can even forget why we started. When really, we need to reconnect with our purpose.

It Starts with You! – Anything Is Possible! Everything starts in the mind before it manifests into a plan so if there is something occurring in your life take a second to think about what you are choosing to focus on and what you are allowing to gain your attention as where your attention goes energy flows and results will show.

Always remember success is never owned, it is merely rented, and the rent is due every single day.

"VALIDATE YOURSELF OTHERWISE YOU'LL SPEND A LIFETIME TRYING TO PROVE YOURSELF TO OTHERS."

"VALIDATE YOURSELF OTHERWISE YOU'LL SPEND A LIFETIME TRYING TO PROVE YOURSELF TO OTHERS."

Dogs were put to compete with a cheetah, the goal was to find out who is faster. Everyone was surprised that the cheetah didn't move out of its place, so they asked the race coordinator what happened?! His response was "Sometimes trying to prove yourself is the worst thing you could possibly do. We don't need to go down to other people's level to make them understand that we are the best. Think hard and save your energy for what you deserve, always remember that the cheetah will only use its speed to hunt dogs not to prove they are faster and stronger than a dog.

DO NOT WASTE YOUR TIME TRYING TO PROVE YOUR VALUE TO PEOPLE WHO WILL NEVER UNDERSTAND

"EVERYTHING WE DO MATTERS FROM THE MUSIC WE LISTEN TO THE PEOPLE WE SURROUND OURSELVES WITH EVERYTHING WE DO EACH AND EVERY DAY EITHER TAKES YOU ONE STEP CLOSER OR FURTHER AWAY FROM YOUR GOALS."

"EVERYTHING WE DO MATTERS FROM THE MUSIC WE LISTEN TO THE PEOPLE WE SURROUND OURSELVES WITH EVERYTHING WE DO EACH AND EVERY DAY EITHER TAKES YOU ONE STEP CLOSER OR FURTHER AWAY FROM YOUR GOAL."

There's always more than one way to achieve the same goal. Take a second to think about this especially on this journey that we call life as at times you may feel as though you have fallen off track, but understand that one chapter that didn't go your way doesn't determine the rest of your story.

Understand how it is, what it is and what has happened; but what's going to happen is within your control. The choices you make and are making are impacting your future, if not immediately then further down the line it most definitely will.

Understand that everything has come to fruition as a result of consistent steps in a set direction so if you desire to work your way towards wealth understand that it won't happen overnight. It will be a journey of having to rewire your mindset as when you are wealthy you thrive in every area of your life.

So, I implore you to take that step today in the right direction and allow yourself to start taking those steps towards wealth creation.

"EVERYTHING STARTS IN THE MIND BEFORE IT MANIFESTS INTO A PLAN. SO, IF THERE IS SOMETHING OCCURING IN YOUR LIFE THAT YOU DO NOT DESIRE, TAKE A SECOND TO THINK ABOUT WHAT YOU ARE FOCUSING ON AS WHERE YOUR ATTENTION GOES, ENERGY FLOWS."

"EVERYTHING STARTS IN THE MIND BEFORE IT MANIFESTS INTO A PLAN. SO, IF THERE IS SOMETHING OCCURING IN YOUR LIFE THAT YOU DO NOT DESIRE, TAKE A SECOND TO THINK ABOUT WHAT YOU ARE FOCUSING ON AS WHERE YOUR ATTENTION GOES, ENERGY FLOWS."

In life some of us tend to get so caught up in acting and constantly striving to put up this front and this whole facade of it all being ok. Sometimes we get so used to wearing this mask that we can't differentiate between the two and actually get so used to living like this that we fool ourselves and actually plummet our own growth.

What people fail to understand at times is that through our vulnerability you are able to grow in an unmeasurable way. As the only limit to where your growth will stop is where you choose for it to do so. Never limit yourself and always be open to change as it is a natural part of life which grants access to a box of limitless possibilities so the next time you are given an opportunity simply take a chance as you never know where it may lead.

I am a huge believer and understand the importance of authenticity and simply showing up as the best version of you.

"LEARN TO BE PROACTIVE AS OPPOSED TO REACTIVE."

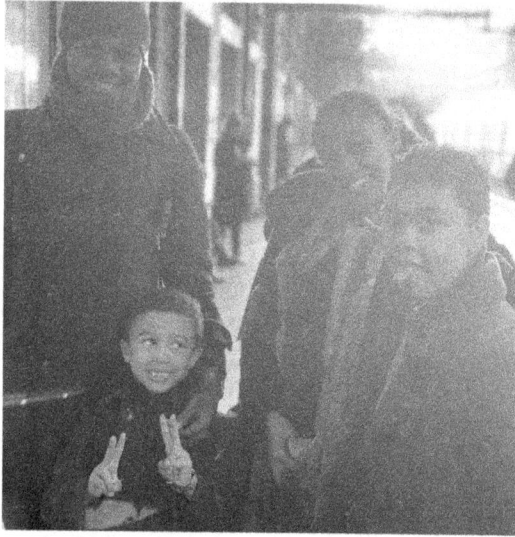

"LEARN TO BE PROACTIVE AS OPPOSED TO REACTIVE."

Sometimes the smallest things can change our lives in the blink of an eye but what matters is what you take from that experience and simply learning to accept it for what it is.

You see sometimes we actually make things seem a lot more complex than they actually are. You may even be unconsciously stopping yourself from growing... from achieving... from success. Learn to trust the process and you'll get there in the end. Sometimes the smallest things can change our lives in the blink of an eye but what matters is what you take from that experience and simply learn to accept it for what it is.

You see sometimes we actually make things seem a lot more complex than they actually are. You may even be unconsciously stopping yourself from growing... from achieving... from success.

Learn to trust the process and you'll get there in the end.

"EVERYTHING IS CONNECTED
IN ONE WAY OR ANOTHER SO
LEARN TO LOOK AT LIFE AS A
LESSON. LEARN TO LISTEN
AND TAKE IT IN OTHERWISE
THE LESSON WILL REPEAT
ITSELF UNTIL YOU DO."

It Starts with You! – Anything Is Possible!

"EVERYTHING IS CONNECTED IN ONE WAY OR ANOTHER SO LEARN TO LOOK AT LIFE AS A LESSON. LEARN TO LISTEN AND TAKE IT IN OTHERWISE THE LESSON WILL REPEAT ITSELF UNTIL YOU DO."

Try to learn everything about one thing and in doing so you'll know something about everything.

In life we tend to focus on 101 things and end up spreading ourselves too thin.

Learn to focus on 1 thing and apply those teachings to different areas of your life.

"I AM NOT A PRODUCT OF MY CIRCUMSTANCE, I AM A PRODUCT OF MY DECISION."

It Starts with You! – Anything Is Possible!

"I AM NOT A PRODUCT OF MY CIRCUMSTANCE, I AM A PRODUCT OF MY DECISION."

You can't change where you start, but you can definitely decide where you choose to finish.

In life, there are some things which let's face it we don't have the power to change, but as life moves on as we evolve we are able to make those decisions that could help to put us in a place of choice(s). So, we are able to live and leave that legacy, and remember 'It all starts with YOU.

"JUST BECAUSE YOU'RE A PIONEER DOESN'T MEAN YOU WILL STAY THERE, YOU HAVE TO KEEP GROWING TO KEEP YOUR PLACE."

"JUST BECAUSE YOU'RE A PIONEER DOESN'T MEAN YOU WILL STAY THERE, YOU HAVE TO KEEP GROWING TO KEEP YOUR PLACE."

Learn to loosen up and comprehend how what was once imperative is now obsolete.

As when it comes to business and maintaining that growth you need to learn to adapt to your surroundings and that is not to say you need to change who you are, it is simply to alternate the way you convey the same message.

So, although the message never actually changed you are now talking in a way your customers will understand.

"HE WHO CAN MANAGE LITTLE
CAN MANAGE MUCH."

It Starts with You! – Anything Is Possible!

"He who can manage little can manage much. Learn to see how all things are connected and how a small problem if overlooked can have grand consequences."

Tray-Sean Ben Salmi
AKA T7

If you can't manage £100, then you can't manage $100,000.

You don't suddenly learn how to handle money by amassing more of it. Hence why a lot of lottery winners lose it all within 5 years.

That's why I am so keen on teaching financial education as it's not just having this money, it's about knowing what to do with it so you own things to pass down your lineage.

Remember that financial literacy is not a side effect of wealth. Wealth is a side effect of financial literacy. Get it right and you can change your life.

"DO TODAY WHAT MOST
PEOPLE WON'T, SO YOU CAN
LIVE TOMORROW LIKE MOST
PEOPLE DON'T."

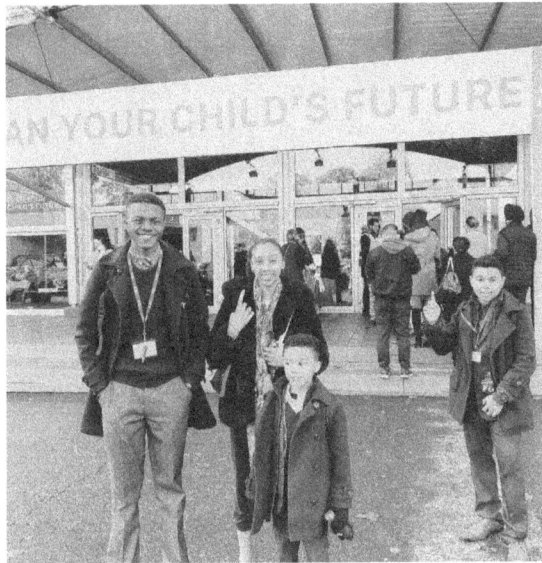

"DO TODAY WHAT MOST PEOPLE WON'T, SO YOU CAN LIVE TOMORROW LIKE MOST PEOPLE DON'T."

You see, in life we are often not scared of failure but of how much we can truly achieve. We are scared about what others may think of us when we make it.

You see we shouldn't let anything hold us back in life, from achieving and living life to the fullest. That way it shows that you are not only able to thrive in life, but you are able to live on purpose and show that you have a mission that you have come to this earth to achieve.

You see, the only thing that can stop you from achieving whatever you set your mind to is the limitations that you have made up in your own mind.

So learn to let go and give it your all..

"YOUR TIME IS LIKE WATER FLOWING IN A RIVER, YOU CANNOT TOUCH THE SAME WATER TWICE BECAUSE WHAT HAS PASSED WILL NEVER PASS AGAIN SO USE YOUR TIME WISELY."

"YOUR TIME IS LIKE WATER FLOWING IN A RIVER, YOU CANNOT TOUCH THE SAME WATER TWICE BECAUSE WHAT HAS PASSED WILL NEVER PASS AGAIN SO USE YOUR TIME WISELY."

If I was to ask you what you value more your time or money?

I'd imagine that you'd say time hopefully anyway.

So, why do so many people trade their time for money. After all, no matter how much money you gave you can never trade that for more time. This is why I often say that money provides you with options that way you are able to work towards attaining freedom.

"A SHIP IS SAFE IN THE HARBOUR, BUT THAT'S NOT WHAT SHIPS ARE FOR. YOU MAY FEEL SAFE IN YOUR COMFORT ZONE, BUT YOU ARE NOT LIVING YOU'RE MERELY SURVIVING. LEARN TO GROW AND BE IN THE MYSTERY."

"A SHIP IS SAFE IN THE HARBOUR BUT THAT'S NOT WHAT SHIPS ARE FOR. YOU MAY FEEL SAFE IN YOUR COMFORT ZONE, BUT YOU ARE NOT LIVING YOU'RE MERELY SURVIVING. LEARN TO GROW AND BE IN THE MYSTERY."

Remember this, as you may feel safe and comfortable where you are, but you are not truly living life, you are merely surviving. Learn to live, learn to thrive, be in the mystery and strive for more.

"LEARN TO ADAPT TO YOUR SURROUNDINGS INSTEAD OF DWELLING ON WHAT ONCE WAS."

"LEARN TO ADAPT TO YOUR SURROUNDINGS INSTEAD OF DWELLING ON WHAT ONCE WAS."

Sometimes the smallest things can change our lives in the blink of an eye, but what matters is what you take from that experienc. Simply learn to accept it for what it is. You see sometimes we actually make things seem a lot more complex than they actually are. You may even be unconsciously stopping yourself from growing... from achieving... from success.

Learn to trust the process and you'll get there in the end.

"ENJOYING YOUR YOUTH
DOESN'T MEAN YOU NEED TO
DESTROY YOUR FUTURE."

"ENJOYING YOUR YOUTH DOESN'T MEAN YOU NEED TO DESTROY YOUR FUTURE."

The choices we make today impact the life we live tomorrow. So, understand the difference between enjoying and squandering as one will make you whereas the other will break you.

Take that first step, start that business, do that workout as change starts with you.

"DREAMS ARE AN INSIGHT OF WHATS AVAILABLE IF YOU TAKE ACTION."

It Starts with You! – Anything Is Possible!

"DREAMS ARE AN INSIGHT OF WHATS AVAILABLE IF YOU TAKE ACTION."

A dream will forever stay that way until you pair it up with **action** and then it shall become a **reality**.

Whatever you put work into will continue to grow so ask yourself what do you focus on and how is that impacting your life?

"WE CANNOT CHOOSE WHERE WE START BUT WE GET TO DECIDE WHERE WE FINISH."

It Starts with You! – Anything Is Possible!

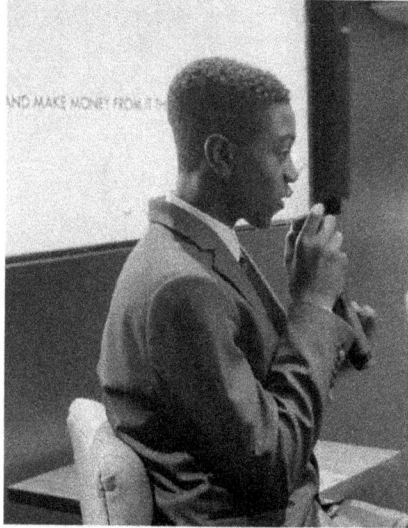

"WE CANNOT CHOOSE WHERE WE START BUT WE GET TO DECIDE WHERE WE FINISH."

Stop procrastinating. Stop waiting for the perfect moment. The time is now. **ACT NOW!...**

How many times have you heard or maybe even said I'm waiting for the perfect time...

I'm not ready yet...

I am going to invest...

I will learn to trade when the time is right...

It Starts with You! – Anything Is Possible!

Take action for your inaction is holding you back from making money, changing your life, inspiring others.

Act now and you'll forever thrive or act last and you'll barely stay alive.

"JEWELLERY IS ONLY AS ELEGANT AS THE PERSON WHO WEARS IT."

"JEWELLERY IS ONLY AS ELEGANT AS THE PERSON WHO WEARS IT."

Understand that things do not change who you are it simply give space to amplify the person you already are. This is the same case with money if you are a generous person you will still be generous however you can now do so even more.

So don't expect external things to affect you internally. One of the first steps in changing is accepting truth. Will you choose to grow?

"STAY TRUE TO YOU AFTER ALL
IT'S BETTER TO HAVE ONE
PERSON BELIEVE IN WHAT YOU
ARE THAN A HUNDRED PEOPLE
BELIVE IN SOMETHING YOU
ARE NOT."

"STAY TRUE TO YOU AFTER ALL IT'S BETTER TO HAVE ONE PERSON BELIEVE IN WHAT YOU ARE THAN A HUNDRED PEOPLE BELIVE IN SOMETHING YOU ARE NOT."

One thing that we often lack in life is congruency and consistency. You see what we tend to do in life is say one thing but do the other.

You see many people tend to say and do rather contradicting things. For example, they may say that you should only eat foods that nourish and look after your body. But then you see them in McDonald's, doesn't add upright?

The main thing that I wanted to share with you and I would like you to gain from this post is that consistency is key. It doesn't matter what market you are in what you stand for as a person/ brand. As long as you have core values and live by them just know that you will succeed in whatever you decide to do.

Another thing that's key and is linked in with consistency is congruency. when you are congruent you simply multiply your levels of success. This is because, when you are congruent everything you indulge in is constantly either in line with your dream, will make you grow or assist others.

By being congruent simply allows you to stay true to the real you. It is about not being afraid to say this is me, this is what I stand for and if you don't agree I'm sorry, but I can't work with you. Being congruent is all about being in alignment and staying on that soul mission and simply maintaining that's the vision of yours and using it to succeed and inspire others to do so too.

"THE FUTURE YOU WILL GO ON TO LIVE IS SHOWN IN YOUR DAILY ROUTINE."

It Starts with You! – Anything Is Possible!

"THE FUTURE YOU WILL GO ON TO LIVE IS SHOWN IN YOUR DAILY ROUTINE."

One thing that everyone should do on a daily basis is read and not only do we learn but we are therefore able to expand and have discussions of meaning.

One of the things which is of great importance in everyday life is the ability to hold a conversation regardless of whom the individual is and by have an array of knowledge you are able to do so with ease so start today!

I know that it can be hard to start but remember that motivation is temperamental whereas discipline lasts a lifetime.

"EVERYTHING WE DO MATTERS."

It Starts with You! – Anything Is Possible!

"EVERYTHING WE DO MATTERS."

From the words we say, things we eat, the clothes we wear to the music we listen to everything goes into the person you are today.

Everything is a choice you can have that meal you have craved for an hour or work towards the body you crave but don't expect anything if you're not willing to put in the work.

This not only applies to you but seek to encourage others in your family to do the same as your only as strong as your weakest link.

"THE ONLY LIMIT TO HOW MUCH YOU CAN ACHIEVE IS THE ONE YOU SET YOURSELF."

"The only limit to your success is the one you set yourself."

- Tray-Sean Ben Salmi

"THE ONLY LIMIT TO HOW MUCH YOU CAN ACHIEVE IS THE ONE YOU SET YOURSELF."

NOTHING IS SET IN STONE

There is nothing that you cannot accomplish. This also applies to how long it will take you to accomplish a goal as Elon Musk has said if you set yourself 3 days to get something done you will do so in 3 days needless to say if you was to set yourself 3 hours to achieve the same outcome you can still achieve it.

Looking back on my eventful life I have come to realise how things that I often did not understand at the time, are now beginning to make sense.

One of the biggest breakthroughs I have had is to do with my breathing as it is something that I always perceived as holding me back. Whereas actually, it has been the test of all tests being able to possess self-control. Being proactive as opposed to reactive.

I will continue to share more about this...

I hope you are able to understand that everything happens for a reason and learn to be grateful.

"GAINING MONEY IS AN
ACTION. MAINTAINING
MONEY IS A BEHAVIOUR.
MULTIPLYING MONEY IS
KNOWLEDGE."

It Starts with You! – Anything Is Possible!

"GAINING MONEY IS AN ACTION.

MAINTAINING MONEY IS A BEHAVIOUR.

MULTIPLYING MONEY IS KNOWLEDGE."

Sometimes in life it's not about reinventing the wheel, it's about simply replicating what works and adjusting everything else to benefit you.

Learn to work smart.

We often believe that a leader has to lead from the front but not in all cases you see leaders are simply the light that allows others to see.

You see in life we tend to believe (due to subliminal messages negative depiction of

It Starts with You! – Anything Is Possible! different genders and race) that leaders have to be the most popular person who knows everyone and everyone is constantly talking about them.

When a true leader is someone who is able to lead no matter where it is from it can be that one person who people may think ⬤ about how they get things done yet they never see them move.

The one thing that defines a leader is being able to protect and guide all in the right place and not being afraid to say that someone is doing a better job than you and that they should take your place.

Leadership is about putting the needs of others above your own ego. Yes, it may sound easy, but it is something that takes time to truly master. You see a leader doesn't even have to know it all they can simply just provide the support and resources to assist. You see a leader get involved in the dream instead of bossing others to do so.

Where a BOSS says " Go "
A LEADER says " Let's GO "

Be a leader because as I always say "Leaders originate, for others to imitate"

You can choose what side you choose to be on because at the end of the day "Either you run the day or the day runs you"

It Starts with You! – Anything Is Possible!

One Day At A Time
Journal

ONE DAY AT A TIME DAILY JOURNAL

Writing things down is an effective way of taking the time to appreciate the amazing things that take place every day. This can also help with achieving your goals by setting your intentions for the day.

No matter how much you write take the time to really think about your day and remember that success doesn't come overnight it is all down to what you do on a daily basis.

Date: __/__/____ Today I am Grateful For...

_____

_____

Quote of The Day

_____

What Are Your Intentions For Today?

_____

_____

_____

It Starts with You! – Anything Is Possible!

During the evening just before going to bed take a moment to reflect on your day then List the 3 successes you had today.

1) _____

_____

_____

2) _____

_____

_____

3) _____

_____

_____

It Starts with You! – Anything Is Possible!

Date: __/__/____ Today I am Grateful For…

_____

_____

Quote of The Day

_____

What Are Your Intentions For Today?

_____

_____

_____

During the evening just before going to bed take a moment to reflect on your day then List the 3 successes you had today.

1) _____

_____

_____

It Starts with You! – Anything Is Possible!

2) _____

_____

_____

3) _____

_____

_____

Date: __/__/_____ Today I am Grateful For...

_____

_____

Quote of The Day

_____

What Are Your Intentions For Today?

_____

_____

_____

During the evening just before going to bed take a moment to reflect on your day then List the 3 successes you had today.

1) _____

_____

_____

2) _____

_____

_____

3) _____

_____

_____

It Starts with You! – Anything Is Possible!

Date: __/__/____ Today I am Grateful For…

_____

_____

Quote of The Day

_____

What Are Your Intentions For Today?

_____

_____

_____

During the evening just before going to bed take a moment to
reflect on your day then List the 3 successes you had today.

1) _____

_____

_____

It Starts with You! – Anything Is Possible!

2) _____

_____

_____

3) _____

_____

_____

Date: __/__/____ Today I am Grateful For...

_____

_____

Quote of The Day

_____

What Are Your Intentions For Today?

_____

_____

It Starts with You! – Anything Is Possible!

During the evening just before going to bed take a moment to reflect on your day then List the 3 successes you had today.

1) _____

_____

_____

2) _____

_____

_____

3) _____

_____

_____

It Starts with You! – Anything Is Possible!

Date: __/__/____ Today I am Grateful For…

_____

_____

Quote of The Day

_____

What Are Your Intentions For Today?

_____

_____

_____

During the evening just before going to bed take a moment to reflect on your day then List the 3 successes you had today.

1) _____

_____

_____

It Starts with You! – Anything Is Possible!

2) _____

_____

_____

3) _____

_____

_____

Date: __/__/____ Today I am Grateful For…

_____

_____

Quote of The Day

_____

It Starts with You! – Anything Is Possible!

What Are Your Intentions For Today?

_____

_____

_____

During the evening just before going to bed take a moment to reflect on your day then List the 3 successes you had today.

1) _____

_____

_____

2) _____

_____

_____

3) _____

_____

_____

It Starts with You! – Anything Is Possible!

Date: __/__/____ Today I am Grateful For…

_____

_____

Quote of The Day

_____

What Are Your Intentions For Today?

_____

_____

_____

During the evening just before going to bed take a moment to reflect on your day then List the 3 successes you had today.

1) _____

_____

_____

It Starts with You! – Anything Is Possible!

2) _____

_____

_____

3) _____

_____

_____

Date: __/__/____ Today I am Grateful For...

_____

_____

Quote of The Day

_____

What Are Your Intentions For Today?

_____

_____

During the evening just before going to bed take a moment to
reflect on your day then List the 3 successes you had today.

1) _____

_____

_____

2) _____

_____

_____

3) _____

_____

_____

It Starts with You! – Anything Is Possible!

Date: __/__/____ Today I am Grateful For…

_____

_____

Quote of The Day

_____

What Are Your Intentions For Today?

_____

_____

_____

During the evening just before going to bed take a moment to
reflect on your day then List the 3 successes you had today.

1) _____

_____

_____

It Starts with You! – Anything Is Possible!

2) _____

_____

_____

3) _____

_____

_____

Date: __/__/____ Today I am Grateful For…

_____

_____

Quote of The Day

_____

What Are Your Intentions For Today?

_____

_____

_____

During the evening just before going to bed take a moment to reflect on your day then List the 3 successes you had today.

1) _____

_____

_____

2) _____

_____

_____

3) _____

_____

_____

It Starts with You! – Anything Is Possible!

Date: __/__/____ Today I am Grateful For...

_____

_____

Quote of The Day

_____

What Are Your Intentions For Today?

_____

_____

_____

During the evening just before going to bed take a moment to reflect on your day then List the 3 successes you had today.

1) _____

_____

_____

It Starts with You! – Anything Is Possible!

2) _____

_____

_____

3) _____

_____

_____

Date: __/__/____ Today I am Grateful For...

_____

_____

Quote of The Day

_____

What Are Your Intentions For Today?

_____

_____

During the evening just before going to bed take a moment to reflect on your day then List the 3 successes you had today.

1) _____

_____

_____

2) _____

_____

_____

3) _____

_____

_____

It Starts with You! – Anything Is Possible!

Date: __/__/____ Today I am Grateful For…

_____

_____

Quote of The Day

_____

What Are Your Intentions For Today?

_____

_____

_____

During the evening just before going to bed take a moment to reflect on your day then List the 3 successes you had today.

1) _____

_____

_____

It Starts with You! – Anything Is Possible!

2) _____

_____

_____

3) _____

_____

_____

Date: __/__/____ Today I am Grateful For...

_____

_____

Quote of The Day

_____

What Are Your Intentions For Today?

_____

_____

During the evening just before going to bed take a moment to reflect on your day then List the 3 successes you had today.

1) _____

_____

_____

2) _____

_____

_____

3) _____

_____

_____

It Starts with You! – Anything Is Possible!

Date: __/__/____ Today I am Grateful For…

_____

_____

Quote of The Day

_____

What Are Your Intentions For Today?

_____

_____

_____

During the evening just before going to bed take a moment to reflect on your day then List the 3 successes you had today.

1) _____

_____

_____

It Starts with You! – Anything Is Possible!

2) _____

_____

_____

3) _____

_____

_____

Date: __/__/____ Today I am Grateful For...

_____

_____

Quote of The Day

_____

What Are Your Intentions For Today?

_____

_____

During the evening just before going to bed take a moment to reflect on your day then List the 3 successes you had today.

1) _____

_____

_____

2) _____

_____

_____

3) _____

_____

_____

It Starts with You! – Anything Is Possible!

YOU'VE GOT THIS!...

It Starts with You! – Anything Is Possible!

A MESSAGE FROM ME TO YOU

I believe in you…

Remember that no matter what others say as long as you stay true to yourself and stay focused on your goals both long-term and short-term you will get there in the end.

So, understand that leaders originate, for others to imitate so make that change and remember it all starts with you. Tray-Sean Ben Salmi.

It Starts with You! – Anything Is Possible!

ABOUT THE AUTHOR

AS SEEN OF TV, RADIO & NEWSPAPERS etc

17yr old Tray-Sean Ben Salmi is a proud Harovian and an Amazon #1 Best Seller & Award-Winning Author, TEDx Talk Speaker, Guest Speaker at Steve & Marjorie Harvey Foundation, Stock & Shares Trader, Property Mentor & Investor, Award winning Public Speaker (Virgin, The Beat You Expo 15,000 attendees) and Child Advocate. Sponsored by Luster Products. Tray-Sean has recently signed a contract with FirstPoint USA ■ for an opportunity to go to America for a full academic and sports scholarship.

Find him on social media platforms here:
https://linktr.ee/traysean

Tray-Sean desires to financially liberate 1 million people by teaching financial literacy.

Tray-Sean was a guest speaker at The Beat You Expo: https://youtu.be/Fz9mErJC8rA where there were 15,000 attendees.

It Starts with You! – Anything Is Possible!

Tray-Sean Ben Salmi is a Host for a show called
The Influencer Show:
https://tray-sean.sounder.fm/show/life-accordin
g-to-tray-sean

Tray-Sean Ben Salmi was headhunted to develop
UnLtd application process.

Tray-Sean Ben Salmi was the youngest to be
funded by UnLtd 2015 at the age of 11.

Tray-Sean was selected for BBC radio national
syndicate interviews to discuss his journey, thanks
to Primrose.

Tray-Sean works in partnership with Brunel
University alongside his four siblings (20yr old
Lashai Ben Salmi, 12yr old Yasmine Ben Salmi,
11yr old Paolo Ben Salmi and 7yr old Amire Ben
Salmi who's the youngest ever STEM ambassador
for Brunel University)

Tray-Sean held his family's signature 2 Day Family
workshop called Dreaming Big Together - Mamas
Secret Recipe at The Hub Chelsea FC

It Starts with You! – Anything Is Possible! Lashai and her family have been acknowledged in the credits of a NEW movie called: How Thoughts Become Things movie promotional link:

Bit.ly/HowThoughtsBecomeThingsMovie2020

Tray-Sean participated in Channel 4 Child Genius 2017 and went on to be recognized as one of the top 20 smartest children in the UK. Tray-Sean went on to be 1 out of 34 boys to be invited to sit papers at the prestigious Eton College 2017.

Tray-Sean is the founder of Influencer Publishing House.

Tray-Sean hosted his signature program called I'm That KID at Virgin Money Lounge

Tray-Sean is an award-winning author of Kidz That Dream Big, Former Radio Show host, Regan Hillyer International Be Your Brand Fellow, Author of 10 Seconds To Child Genius: https://www.lutontoday.co.uk/education/unlock-the-secrets-of-maths-with-luton-s-10-seconds-to-c hild-genius-team-1-9141742, Winner of TruLittle Heros Award – Academic and a Business/Personal developments mentor/coach.

It Starts with You! – Anything Is Possible!

Tray-Sean co-hosted a workshop with his mentor Juergen at Chelsea F.C Foundation & Virgin Money Lounge: https://www.eventbrite.co.uk/e/im-that-kid-trading-made-easy-for-teens-co-hosted-by-14yr-old-tray-sean-ben-salmi-jurgen-pallien-tickets-62663672732

Tray-Sean has participated in brand campaigns for Sainsburys, Legoland, Warner Bros, Sony and Official Judges for Made for Mums Toy Awards to name a few.
Tray-Sean is founder of I'm That KID covers:

- I'm That KID - Bridging the Gap Between Fathers & Sons**TM**

- I'm That KID – Creating A Vision Board for My Future**TM**

- I'm That KID – Taking the Stage**TM**

- I'm That KID - Inspiring My Community to Pay It Forward**TM**

- I'm That KID - There's A Book Inside ME**TM**

It Starts with You! – Anything Is Possible!
- I'm That KID - Families That Play Together
Stay Together**TM**

- I'm That KID - Empowering You to Step Into
Your POWER**TM**

- I'm That KID - BEING the Change That I
Desires To See In The World**TM**

10 Seconds to Child Genius is a book series
co-founded by Tray-Sean Ben Salmi & Philip
Chan. This book series aims to help children and
young people to plant the seed today to create a
brighter future tomorrow.

Q: How do you know what you DON'T KNOW?
A: When someone point out the obvious which
you have overlooked!

There is a mis-conception that only a limited
amount of people can be a 'Child Genius'. In this
book Tray-Sean Ben Salmi show you this 'myth' is
not true.

JUST KNOW THAT YOU CAN HELP YOUR
CHILD TO DISCOVER THEIR GENIUS
WITHIN.

It Starts with You! – Anything Is Possible! Tray-Sean's signature program: I'M That KID Blueprint**TM**

Tray-Sean's Books:

1. 10 Seconds To Child Genius
https://www.amazon.co.uk/dp/099286948X/ref=cm_sw_r_cp_api_uxbUAbPH5C3K1

2. I'm That KID: Empowering You to Step Into Your Power
https://www.amazon.co.uk/dp/B07PXFS7TY/ref=cm_sw_r_cp_api_i_TGZKCb0188EG1

3. 10 Seconds To Child Genius: The Road To Child Genius
https://www.amazon.co.uk/dp/B07PXBS2MQ/ref=cm_sw_r_cp_api_i_CIZKCbDFPKRF7

4. 10 Seconds To Child Genius: From Eton Road To Eton College
https://www.amazon.co.uk/dp/B07P9K469N/ref=cm_sw_r_cp_api_i_rJZKCb951S2FV

5. Kidz That Dream Big!...
https://www.amazon.co.uk/dp/1909039322/ref=cm_sw_r_cp_api_i_-JZKCbYJFFCAD

It Starts with You! – Anything Is Possible!

6. Kidz That Dream Big: Dreams Do Come True
https://www.amazon.co.uk/dp/1912547066/ref=
cm_sw_r_cp_api_i_9KZKCbD0XTRYA

7. Property Problem Solver: Has Your Property
Become   A   Pain   In   Your   Life?
https://www.amazon.co.uk/dp/B07Q7WX3MY/
ref=cm_sw_r_cp_api_i_1cGOCb2XT7BEP

8 10 Seconds To Child Genius: Part Two
https://www.amazon.co.uk/dp/1913310140/ref=
cm_sw_r_cp_api_i_GZt2DbWG9MPM8

9 10 Seconds to Child Genius: From Eton Road
to   Eton   College   Part   2
https://www.amazon.co.uk/dp/1913310108/ref=
cm_sw_r_cp_api_i_u3t2Db1S7QMHY

10 I'm That KID: Empowering You To Step Into
Your   Power   Part   Two
https://www.amazon.co.uk/dp/1913310086/ref=
cm_sw_r_cp_api_i_i4t2DbVQDBY48

11 10 SECONDS TO CHILD GENIUS: THE
ROAD   TO   CHILD   GENIUS   Part   Two
https://www.amazon.co.uk/dp/1913310124/ref=
cm_sw_r_cp_api_i_X4t2DbZAPR808

It Starts with You! – Anything Is Possible!
12 Property Problem Solver: Has Your Property Become A Pain In Your Life? Part Two
https://www.amazon.co.uk/dp/191331006X/ref=cm_sw_r_cp_api_i_.5t2Db2B03DPQ

13 I'm That KID: Trading Made Easy for Teens (2)
https://www.amazon.co.uk/dp/1913310221/ref=cm_sw_r_cp_api_i_F7t2Db7CJMN79

Facebook page: 10 Seconds To Child Genius:
https://m.facebook.com/10secondstochildgenius/

It Starts with You! – Anything Is Possible!

BEN SALMI FAMILY MANTRA

"BEN SALMI TEAMWORK MAKES THE DREAMWORK

We believe that there is no such thing as failure only feedback.

We also believe that the journey of one thousand miles begins with a single step in the right direction

FAMILY ANTHEM

If you want to be somebody,
If you want to go somewhere,
You better wake up and PAY ATTENTION
I'm ready to be somebody,
I'm ready to go somewhere,
I'm ready to wake up and PAY ATTENTION!

The question is ARE **YOU**?

www.ingramcontent.com/pod-product-compliance
Lightning Source LLC
Chambersburg PA
CBHW051225200326
41519CB00025B/7254